"My Phone Was in the Fridge."

A Hilarious Collection of Senior (and Not So Senior) Moments,
Plus Journal Space for You to Write Your Own!

What's This Book About?

Remember when your parents would say they were having a "senior moment" when they couldn't find their keys?

As it turns out, you don't have to be a senior to do this. Living in an age of multi-tasking has apparently fried our brains to the point where people in their twenties are looking for their phone… while they are on the phone.

This is a collection of "senior moments" experienced by people of all ages. Hopefully they will make you laugh and feel better about how you're doing in life.

When you're done reading them, we've also provided you with some space to make your own collection, either of your own moments or those of friends and relatives. Keep this book and refer back to it for years to come!

"Yesterday I was looking for my phone… while I was talking on my phone."

"Went through the drive-through window, paid, waited...

then left without my food."

"Searched for my
glasses
for a full hour…

found all three pairs
on my head."

"Tried to unlock my
front door
with my car keys.
This happens once a week."

"Bought a bottle of
vitamins at Costco.
I was struggling to
read the label,
so I put my thumb and
my forefinger
on the label and tried
to zoom in by
dragging my fingers
across the label.

It did not work."

"Went to fold the laundry after
the
buzzer went off for the dryer.

Discovered dryer was empty,
wet clothes still in the washer.

Have done this three times."

"Left my car running with the keys in it.

In the long-term parking at the airport.

Realized this when I landed at my destination."

"Tried to unlock my
front door
with my car keys.
This happens once a week."

"Got home from the grocery store, started unloading.

Realized I had paid for and brought home all of the stuff in someone else's cart."

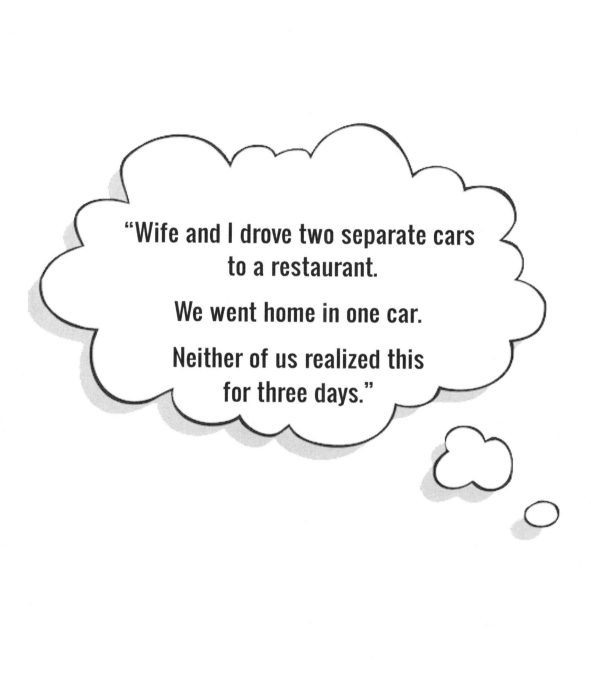

"Made banana bread.

Once it had cooked, cooled, and I cut a piece to taste it,

I realized I had forgotten to put bananas in the banana bread."

"Went out into the parking lot after shopping at the mall. Car was gone. Filed a report with mall security, called the police and the insurance company.

Remembered that the car was parked one floor up."

"I used a magnifying glass to read my iPhone."

"A friend offered to drive me home from event.
We got into the car, drove for about ten minutes,
then realized... it wasn't his car.

We had gotten into a car that was not only
an identical model, but his key fob
had successfully started it."

"Went to check my pulse on my Apple Watch before starting my workout at the gym.

Started to panic when I saw that it was 99. Seriously considered leaving the gym and going to a doctor.

Realized I was looking at the battery percentage."

"Currently staring at lime and coriander on my counter. Does anyone know what I might be making?"

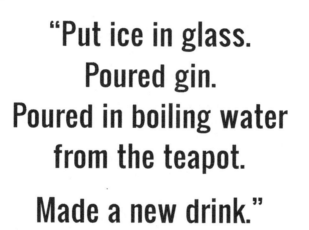

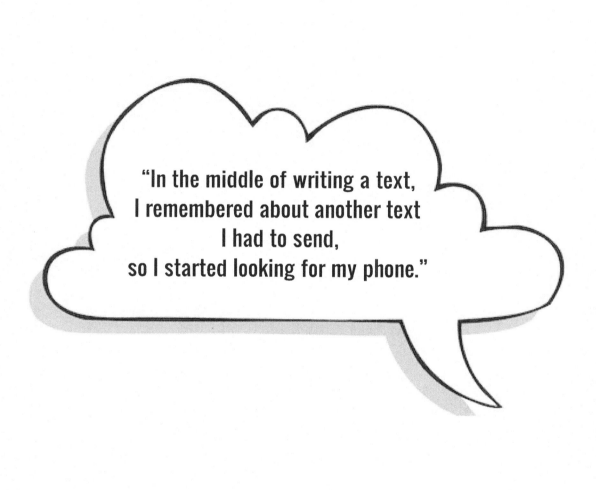

"Went to work.
Worked the whole day.
Checked the schedule to
see when I worked next.

Realized I had just worked
8 hours on my day off."

"Went to the microwave to get the heated-up water for my tea.

Realized I had not put water in the cup."

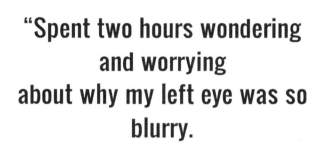

"Texted a friend, 'Hey, did I leave my jacket at your house?'

Got annoyed that he didn't answer.

Realized I had sent a tweet instead of a text.

The internet also did not know where my jacket was."

"Turned on the oven, turned the timer on,
waited for the food to cook.

Realized I did not actually put the food in the oven."

Now, Add Your Own!

You've probably already thought of some of your best (not so) senior moments, and here is where you can those down, so you can laugh at them later!

Every single person you know has done one of these (or something similar), and this is where you can start a hilarious collection. Here are a couple of ways you might want to do that:

- Get this book out the next time you're with a group of friends or at a family gathering, read a few, and then let people start talking. Write down what they say!

- Start a post on your social media, asking people to share their funniest moments. You'll be pleasantly surprised!